ALL ABOUT
Coding Functions

BY JACLYN JAYCOX

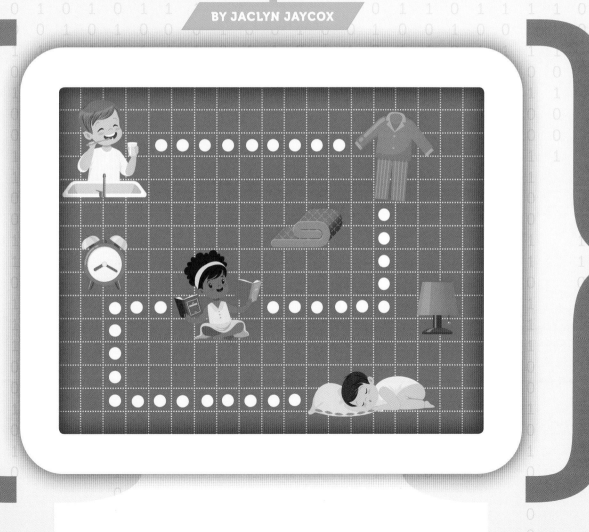

The Child's World®
childsworld.com

Published by The Child's World®
1980 Lookout Drive • Mankato, MN 56003-1705
800-599-READ • www.childsworld.com

Photographs ©: Shutterstock Images, cover (boy
brushing teeth), cover (sleeping boy), cover
(pajamas), cover (towel), cover (clock), cover (lamp),
cover (girl), 1 (boy brushing teeth), 1 (sleeping boy),
1 (pajamas), 1 (towel), 1 (clock), 1 (lamp), 1 (girl),
5, 7, 9, 10, 14, 24; Wave Break Media/Shutterstock
Images, 17; SFC/Shutterstock Images, 18

ISBN 9781503831995
LCCN 2018962820

Printed in the United States of America
PA02418

ABOUT THE AUTHOR

Jaclyn Jaycox is a children's book writer and editor. When she's not writing, Jaclyn loves drinking coffee, reading, and spending time with her family. She lives in southern Minnesota with her husband, two kids, and naughty German shepherd.

TABLE OF CONTENTS

Chapter 1 **What Is a Function?** . . . 4

Chapter 2 **Parts of a Function** . . . 8

Chapter 3 **Why Use Functions?** . . . 12

Chapter 4 **More Ways to Use Functions** . . . 16

DO YOU KNOW? . . . 20

GLOSSARY . . . 22

TO LEARN MORE . . . 23

INDEX . . . 24

What Is a Function?

It is late. Jamie's mom tells her to go put on her pajamas. Jamie puts on her pink pajamas. Jamie's mom then tells her to brush her teeth. Jamie brushes her teeth. Finally, Jamie's mom tells her to pick out a bedtime story. Jamie picks her favorite story. Now, Jamie is all ready for bed.

The next night, Jamie's mom tells Jamie to get ready for bed. This time, Jamie knows what to do. She goes and puts on her pajamas, brushes her teeth, and picks out a bedtime story. Jamie's mom only has to tell her what to do once because Jamie has learned all the instructions for getting ready for bed.

Jamie knows that "Get ready for bed" means to put on her pajamas, brush her teeth, and pick out a bedtime story.

5

Computers can learn sets of instructions, too. These sets are called **functions**. Functions are one of the building blocks of computer **code**. Code is a list of instructions that tell a computer what to do. A function combines a set of instructions into a single command. This command can be reused later. The next time a **coder** wants the computer to follow those instructions, she only needs to type the command.

Once Jamie learned the command "Get ready for bed," she only needed to be given one command instead of three.

Put on pajamas

↓

Brush your teeth

↓

Pick out a bedtime story

↓

Jamie is ready for bed!

Function: Get ready for bed {put on pajamas, brush your teeth, pick out a story}

↓

Jamie is ready for bed!

CHAPTER 2

Parts of a Function

There are four parts of a function. The first part is the name. After coders decide what a function will do, they give it a name. The name is used to **call** the function later. The name of a function lets coders use it again as many times as they want. Names also allow coders to use functions they did not write themselves. Many programs have a library of functions to choose from.

Libraries of functions let people use functions that they did not code themselves.

The second part of a function is the **input**. The input is what the function will work on. Not all functions have an input. The third part of the function is the body. The body is where the instructions are. These instructions take the input and create the **output**. The output is the last part of a function. For example, a coder could write a function that would double any input. If the input is 10, then the output would be 20.

```
function doubleNumber (10) {
      double_input
}

               --output = 20
```

In the example above, the word *function* marks the beginning of the function. The name goes next. This function's name is doubleNumber. The input goes between parentheses. Here, the input is 10. Curly braces mark the body. Inside the curly braces is where the instructions for the function go. The output for this function is 20.

CHAPTER 3

Why Use Functions?

Functions make coding much simpler. Thanks to functions, coders don't have to type the same code over and over again. When writing code, coders want to keep their code DRY. DRY means Don't Repeat Yourself. Keeping code DRY prevents a program from becoming too difficult and saves space. DRY code also reduces the chances for mistakes. The opposite of DRY code is WET code, which stands for Write Everything Twice. Coders try to avoid WET code because it is too long and hard to write. Coders use functions to make code DRY.

WET VS. DRY CODE

A coder creates a function to tell the computer to print "You are great!" and then send an alert that says, "I think you are great!" He names it printAndAlert. Now, if he wants the computer to do this more than once, then he only needs to type out the function's name instead of the whole code.

WET Code

```
print ("You are great!");
alert ("I think you are great!");
print ("You are great!");
alert ("I think you are great!");
print ("You are great!");
alert ("I think you are great!");
```

DRY Code

```
printAndAlert();
printAndAlert();
printAndAlert();
```

```javascript
        }
    ze.no_json || (ce.XHR = $.ajax({
        url: ce.json_url + "?" + $.par
```

When functions get too long, coders break them up into sub-functions.

```javascript
        dataType: "json"
    }).done(function(Re) {
        xe(Re)
    }).fail(function() {
        console.warn("ajax of3 fail")
    }).always(function() {
        $("#lay_" + Oe).removeClass("l
    })), $(".mmi").removeClass("mmi-ac
        "mmi-active"), "user" == ze.nai
    getNested(we, "uid") && ($(".mmi")
        ".mmi-profile").addClass("mmi-
        Re, Se) {
        Se(Oe)
    }), ze.template && ze.no_json && x

}

function o(ye) {
    for (var we = "", be =
        "ABCDEFGHIJKLMNOPQRSTUVWXYZabc
    ye; ke++) we += be.charAt(Math.flo
    return we
}

function r() {
    return {
        type: null,
        detail: null,
        view_mode: null,
        sort: null,
        count: null,
        filters: null,
        q: null
```

```javascript
    }).always(function(Ae) {
        Ae = L(Ae), xe.always(Ae)
    })
}

function S(ye) {
    "function" != typeof ye && (ye = f
    var we = $("html, body");
    we.stop().animate({
        scrollTop: 0
    }, 500, "swing", function() {
        ye()
    })
}

function U() {
    var ye = $("#prof").val(),
        we = $(".model-specs");
    we.removeClass("mpaaf-modelfemale"
        "modelfemale" == ye ? we.addCl
        we.addClass("mpaaf-modelmale")
}

function P(ye) {
    var we =

        /^(([^<>()\[\]\.,;:\s@\"]+(\.
        "]+\.)+[^<>()[\]\.,;:\s@\"]{2,
    return we.test(ye)
}

function T(ye, we) {
    var be = {};
    try {
        be = JSON.parse(ye.data("deta
    } catch (ke) {}
    return "undefined" == typeof we ?
}

function L(ye) {
    if ("object" != typeof ye) try {
        ye = JSON.parse(ye)
    } catch (we) {
```

Sometimes coders need to change parts of their code. If they use functions, then they only have to make the change in one place. If they don't use functions, then they have to make the change in many different places. If coders forget to make a change somewhere, their programs may not work.

Sometimes functions can get too long and confusing. When this happens, coders split them up into smaller functions, called sub-functions.

CHAPTER 4

More Ways to Use Functions

Functions replace code that is used more than once in a program. But there are other times when functions can be helpful. Many websites use functions. Suppose a boy named Dillon signs into a website he uses at school. After he signs in, there is a greeting at the top of the page that says "Welcome, Dillon!" This is done using a function. The input is Dillon's name. The function tells the computer to say welcome to whomever signs onto the website.

Websites use functions to display personal greetings.

17

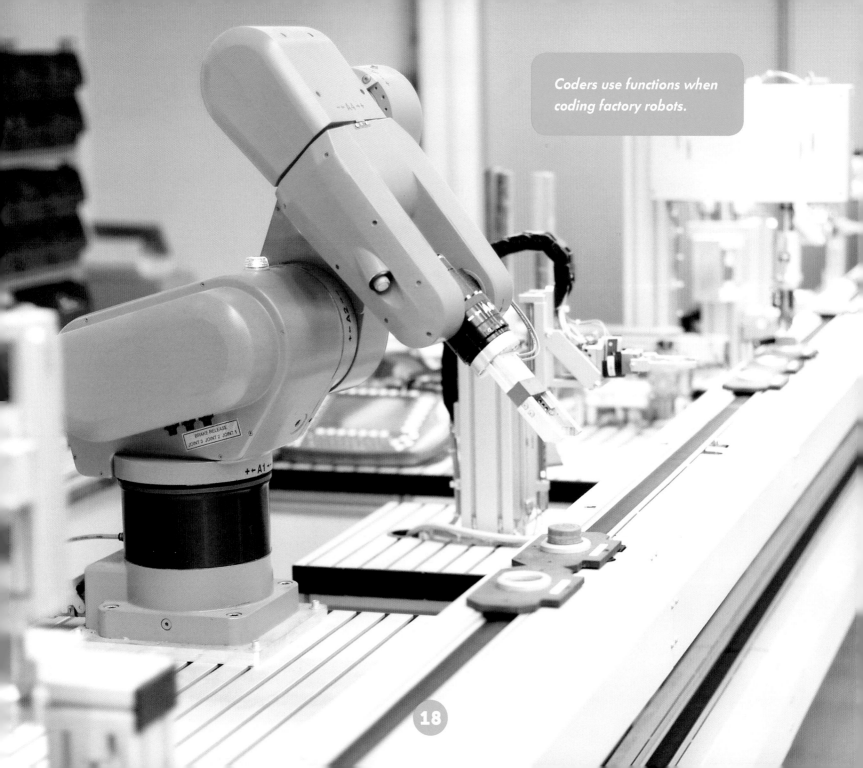

Coders use functions when coding factory robots.

Functions are also useful for coding robots. Some robots are used in toy factories. One of their jobs is to put each toy into a box. This job requires many actions, such as picking up a toy, moving it, and setting it in a box. Each action requires different sets of code. A coder could create a function for each action. That way, when the robot needs to repeat the job, the coder only has to write the function names for each action instead of the full code.

There are endless possibilities when it comes to computer coding. Functions are a key part of making coding simpler.

Q: What is a function?

    a. a part of code that can only be used once

    b. an input

    c. a set of instructions that can be reused

    d. a mistake

A: c. a set of instructions that can be reused

Q: What does DRY stand for? Why is it usually best to keep code DRY?

A: DRY stands for Don't Repeat Yourself. It makes coding easier, saves space, and reduces mistakes.

Q: Which of these is not a part of a function?

    a. input

    b. body

    c. name

    d. sub-function

A: d. sub-function

Q: What are some different ways to use functions?

A: Functions can be used for displaying website greetings and coding robots.

GLOSSARY

call (KAHL) To call a function means to use a function that has already been named. A coder must call a function to use it in the code.

code (KOHD) Code is a list of instructions that computers follow to do things. Robots follow code.

coder (KOHD-ur) A coder is someone who writes code. A coder uses functions when writing code.

functions (FUHNK-shuhnz) Functions are sets of instructions in computer code that can be reused. Functions make computer code easier to write.

input (IN-put) An input is information put into a function. A function works on the input.

output (OUT-put) An output is the information a computer produces. A function produces an output from the input.

sub-functions (SUB-FUHNK-shuhnz) Sub-functions are smaller functions inside a larger function. Coders split functions that are too long into sub-functions.

IN THE LIBRARY

Claybourne, Anna. *Coding and Computers*.
Bath, UK: Parragon, 2016.

Kelly, James Floyd. *The Story of Coding*.
New York, NY: DK Publishing, 2017.

Kulz, George Anthony. *How to Read Scratch Computer Code*. Mankato, MN: The Child's World, 2018.

ON THE WEB

Visit our website for links about coding:
childsworld.com/links

INDEX

body, 10–11

command, 6–7

DRY code, 12–13

input, 10–11, 16
instructions, 4, 6, 10–11

names, 8, 11, 13, 19

output, 10–11

robots, 19

sub-functions, 15

websites, 16
WET code, 12–13